A CONTINENT OF CREATURES

The Animals of
NORTH AMERICA

Amie Jane Leavitt

PURPLE TOAD
PUBLISHING

Banff National Park is a beautiful forested area of Canada.

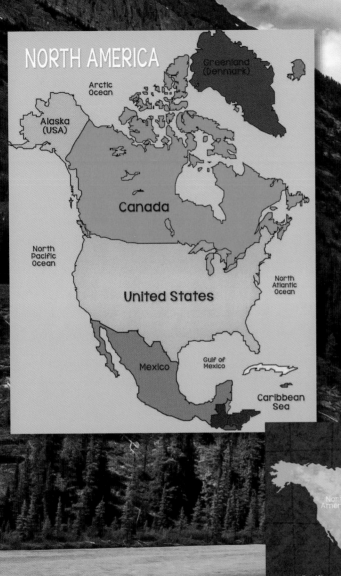

NORTH AMERICA

Arctic Ocean

Greenland (Denmark)

Alaska (USA)

Canada

North Pacific Ocean

United States

North Atlantic Ocean

Mexico

Gulf of Mexico

Caribbean Sea

North America

Europe

Asia

Atlantic Ocean

Africa

Pacific Ocean

South America

Indian Ocean

Australia

Antarctica

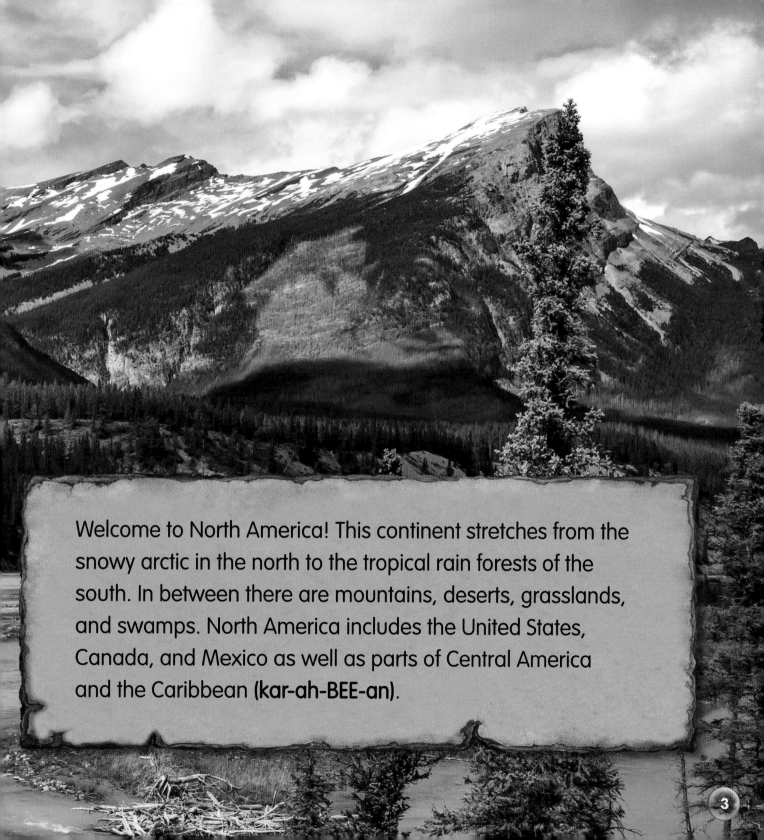

Welcome to North America! This continent stretches from the snowy arctic in the north to the tropical rain forests of the south. In between there are mountains, deserts, grasslands, and swamps. North America includes the United States, Canada, and Mexico as well as parts of Central America and the Caribbean (kar-ah-BEE-an).

The Joshua tree grows 20 to 70 feet tall.

Part of North America is made up of desert land. A desert is dry and home to many plants and animals.

Flowers, cactuses, and even Joshua trees live in the desert. It's the perfect place for lizards, tortoises, snakes, jackrabbits, roadrunners, mountain lions, and a lot of insects.

The Gila (HEE-lah) monster is the biggest lizard in the desert. Gilas are two feet long and weigh five pounds. They have a black body with yellow, orange, or pink patterns.

Jackrabbits also live in the desert. Heat leaves their bodies through their big ears, keeping them cool.

Jackrabbits sprint up to 40 miles per hour.

The Gila monster

Just north and east of the American desert are the Great Plains. These plains are known as the "breadbasket" of America because so much grain grows there.

Many kinds of animals live on the plains. Prairie (PRAYR-ee) dogs burrow under the soil, and deer dine on prairie grasses. Grasshoppers blend into green or brown leaves.

Prairie dogs live in close family groups.

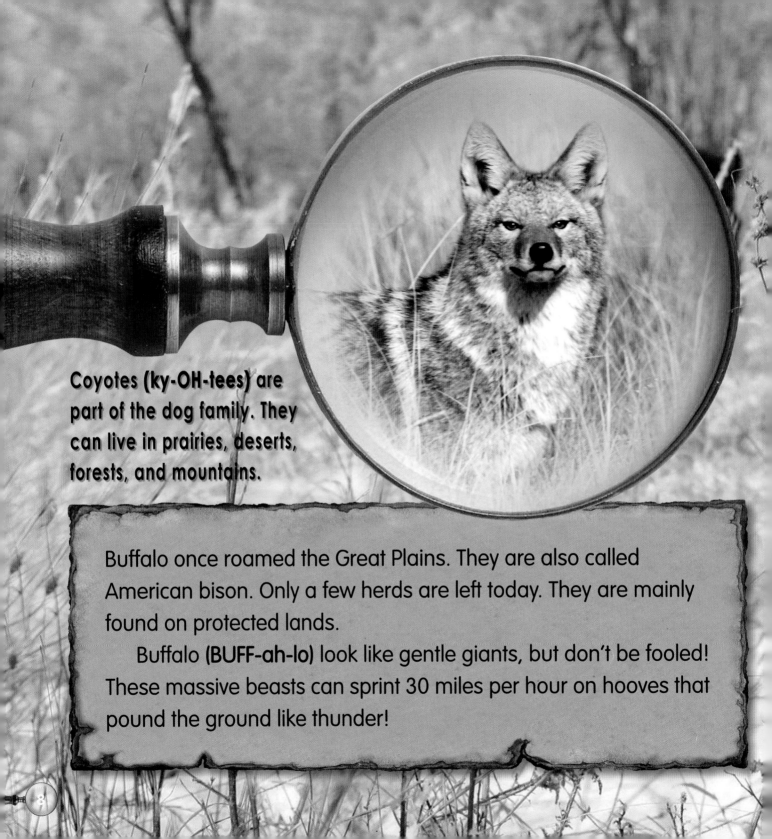

Coyotes (ky-OH-tees) are part of the dog family. They can live in prairies, deserts, forests, and mountains.

Buffalo once roamed the Great Plains. They are also called American bison. Only a few herds are left today. They are mainly found on protected lands.

Buffalo (BUFF-ah-lo) look like gentle giants, but don't be fooled! These massive beasts can sprint 30 miles per hour on hooves that pound the ground like thunder!

Bison can grow to be 12 feet long.

Bald eagles live in large nests made of sticks. Some nests can weigh as much as a small car.

The bald eagle is America's national bird. Born with all brown feathers, it gets its head of white feathers by age five. Bald eagles make their large nests high in tall trees. The largest nest found was 9½ feet wide and 20 feet high. Bald eagles use the nests over and over.

Soaring high above the trees at night is the spotted owl. Hoot, hoot! The owl eats small mammals and other birds and makes its home in tree hollows.

The great horned owl has puffs of feathers on its head that look like horns. This is the most common owl in North America.

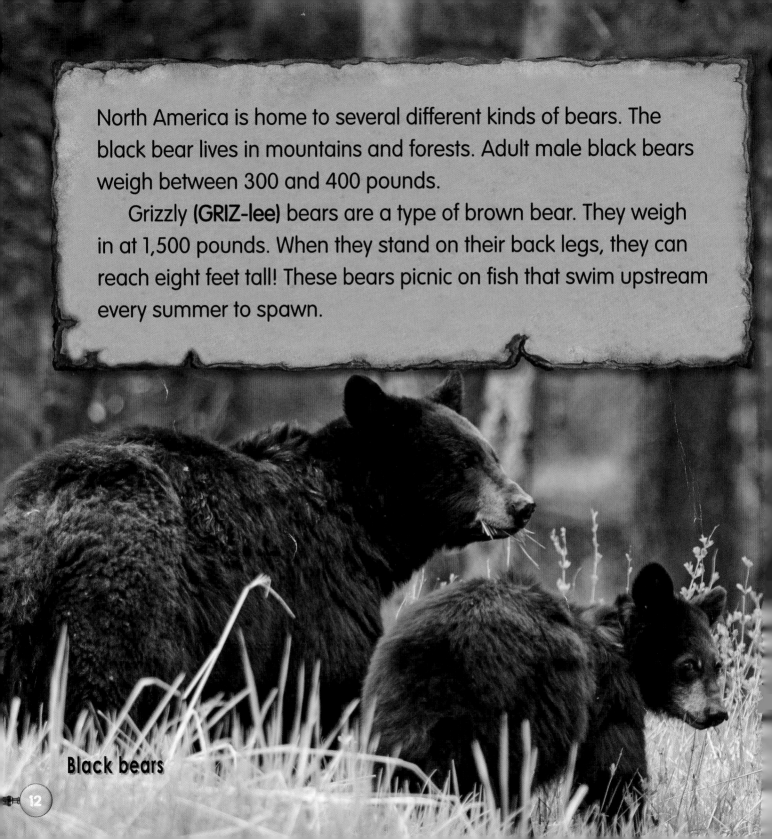

North America is home to several different kinds of bears. The black bear lives in mountains and forests. Adult male black bears weigh between 300 and 400 pounds.

Grizzly **(GRIZ-lee)** bears are a type of brown bear. They weigh in at 1,500 pounds. When they stand on their back legs, they can reach eight feet tall! These bears picnic on fish that swim upstream every summer to spawn.

Black bears

Grizzlies have humps on their backs made of muscle.

Polar (POH-lar) bears live in North America's very cold arctic area. Their thick fur and a layer of blubber under their skin keeps them warm. When polar bears swim, they close their nose so water doesn't get inside.

Moose are huge animals. Moose can be over six feet tall at the shoulder. Their antlers, or "paddles," are used for fighting. Moose shed their antlers every year.

If you travel toward the North Pole, you'll see both moose and polar bears.

Alligators make small ponds called alligator holes. These holes hold water during dry seasons and can be homes to other animals.

The cottonmouth snake

The American alligator **(AL-ah-gayt-or)** lives in North America's swamps. These chomping reptiles spend their days creeping along the waterways looking like bumpy brown logs. This helps them sneak up on their prey. Its nose is turned upward so it can breathe when it is hiding in the water. Males can be 12 feet long and weigh 1,000 pounds.

The cottonmouth snake is this area's only venomous water snake. It grows up to four feet long and rarely bites humans.

The Monarch
(MON-ark)
butterfly

Some creatures move across the entire continent. The Monarch butterfly spends summers in Canada and California. It spends spring in the middle of the United States and winters in central Mexico. Monarchs have the longest known migration of any insect species.

Lobsters have 10 legs. They crawl on the ocean floor looking for food.

Blue crabs eat plants and animals.

Maine lobsters and Maryland blue crabs live in the oceans around North America. Maryland blue crabs are excellent swimmers. Their back legs work as paddles as they move through the water.

The beaver builds its home in North American streams. White-tailed deer run across tall grasses. People travel all over North America. Everywhere they go, they find new animals to meet!

Beavers live near water. White-tailed deer live in mountains, forests, and plains.

FURTHER READING

Books

De Seve, Karen. *National Geographic Kids Mission: Polar Bear Rescue: All About Polar Bears and How to Save Them*. Washington, D.C.: NG Kids Mission: Animal Rescue, 2014.

Ganeri, Anita. *Gila Monster (A Day in the Life: Desert Animals)*. New York: Heinemann, 2011.

George, Jean Craighead. *The Buffalo Are Back*. New York: Dutton Books for Young Readers, 2010.

Marsh, Laura. *Alligators and Crocodiles*. Washington, D.C.: National Geographic Kids, 2015.

Widman, William. *Owls For Kids: A Children's Book About Owls, Owl Facts, Life, and Pictures*. Amazon Digital Services, 2015.

Web Sites

Crittercam: Arctic Adventure
http://animals.nationalgeographic.com/animals/crittercam-virtual-world-arctic/

National Geographic: Animals
http://animals.nationalgeographic.com/

The San Diego Zoo: North America
http://animals.sandiegozoo.org/regions/north-america

Smithsonian's National Zoo
https://nationalzoo.si.edu

adapt (ah-DAPT)—To change in order to survive in a place.

arctic (ARK-tik)—Very cold areas near Earth's north and south poles.

blubber (BLUH-bur)—A layer of fat that grows right under the skin that helps to keep an animal warm.

burrow (BUR-oh)—To dig a hole or tunnel in the ground.

camouflage (KAM-uh-flahj)—The ability to blend in with the color of your environment.

desolate (DEH-soh-lit)—Empty of life.

hollow (HAH-loh)—A hole in a tree or rock.

migration (my-GRAY-shun)—A route taken every year from one's winter home to one's summer home, and back.

spawn (SPAWN)—To release and deposit eggs.

venom (VEH-num)—Poison produced by animals.

PHOTO CREDITS: Cover—Denali National Park and Preserve; p. 1—Tambako the Jaguar; p. 2—Sheila Sund ; p. 4—Vicente Villamon, Nefci; p. 6—Tupulak; pp. 8, 21—USFWS Midwest; pp.8, 10—NPS.gov; p. 8—Chris Parker; p. 12—Public Domain, Gregory Smith; p. 17—LtShears; p. 18—DocentJoyce; p. 19—Steven Johnson, Jarek Tuszynski. All other photos—Public Domain. Every measure has been taken to find all copyright holders of material used in this book. In the event any mistakes or omissions have happened within, attempts to correct them will be made in future editions of the book.

INDEX

Printing 1   2   3   4   5   6   7   8   9

The Animals of Africa
The Animals of Antarctica
The Animals of Asia
The Animals of Australia
The Animals of Europe
The Animals of North America
The Animals of South America

ABOUT THE AUTHOR: Amie Jane Leavitt graduated from Brigham Young University and is an accomplished author, researcher, and photographer. She has written more than sixty books for kids, has contributed to online and print media, and has worked as a consultant, writer, and editor for numerous educational publishing and assessment companies. To check out a listing of Amie's current projects and published works, visit her website at www.amiejaneleavitt.com.

Publisher's Cataloging-in-Publication Data
Leavitt, Amie Jane.
   North America / written by Amie Jane Leavitt.
      p. cm.
Includes bibliographic references, glossary, and index.
ISBN 9781624692703
1. Animals—North America—Juvenile literature. I. Series: A continent of creatures.
   QL151 2017
   591.97
Library of Congress Control Number: 2016937186
eBook ISBN: 9781624692710